50 Sugar-Free Dessert Recipes for Home

By: Kelly Johnson

Table of Contents

- Sugar-Free Chocolate Avocado Mousse
- Almond Flour Brownies
- Chia Seed Pudding with Coconut Milk
- Sugar-Free Peanut Butter Cookies
- Keto Cheesecake Bites
- Dark Chocolate Coconut Truffles
- Banana Oatmeal Cookies
- Sugar-Free Carrot Cake
- Berry Chia Jam Bars
- No-Bake Coconut Macaroons
- Flourless Almond Butter Cookies
- Sugar-Free Lemon Bars
- Cinnamon Baked Apples
- Chocolate Chia Pudding
- Sugar-Free Pumpkin Pie
- Keto Chocolate Mug Cake
- Sugar-Free Raspberry Sorbet
- Almond Butter Fudge
- Sugar-Free Vanilla Panna Cotta
- Cacao Energy Bites
- Avocado Chocolate Fudge
- Strawberry Coconut Popsicles
- Peanut Butter Protein Balls
- Sugar-Free Apple Crisp
- No-Bake Cashew Cheesecake
- Sugar-Free Matcha Ice Cream
- Dark Chocolate Almond Bark
- Vegan Sugar-Free Banana Ice Cream
- Chia Flaxseed Crackers with Berries
- No-Bake Oatmeal Protein Bars
- Sugar-Free Chocolate Zucchini Cake
- Cinnamon Walnut Muffins
- Keto Pecan Pie Bars
- Coconut Almond Bliss Balls
- Baked Pears with Walnuts

- Sugar-Free Mocha Mousse
- Pumpkin Spice Energy Bites
- Lemon Coconut Fat Bombs
- Blackberry Almond Tarts
- Sugar-Free Chocolate Pudding
- Sugar-Free Peanut Butter Blondies
- Mango Coconut Cream Dessert
- Keto Snickerdoodle Cookies
- Sugar-Free Tiramisu
- Sugar-Free Vanilla Ice Cream
- Blueberry Almond Butter Cups
- Chocolate Coconut Chia Bars
- Sugar-Free Cranberry Orange Muffins
- Sugar-Free Chocolate Chip Cookies
- Sugar-Free Hazelnut Fudge

Sugar-Free Chocolate Avocado Mousse

Ingredients:

- 2 ripe avocados
- ¼ cup (25g) unsweetened cocoa powder
- ¼ cup (60ml) unsweetened almond milk
- 2 tablespoons sugar-free sweetener
- 1 teaspoon vanilla extract

Instructions:

1. **Blend Ingredients:** Mix all ingredients in a blender until smooth.
2. **Chill & Serve:** Refrigerate for 30 minutes before serving.

Almond Flour Brownies

Ingredients:

- 1 cup (100g) almond flour
- ¼ cup (25g) unsweetened cocoa powder
- ½ teaspoon baking soda
- ½ cup (120ml) melted coconut oil
- ¼ cup (60ml) sugar-free sweetener
- 2 eggs
- 1 teaspoon vanilla extract

Instructions:

1. **Mix Dry Ingredients:** Combine almond flour, cocoa powder, and baking soda.
2. **Add Wet Ingredients:** Stir in coconut oil, sweetener, eggs, and vanilla.
3. **Bake:** Pour into a greased pan and bake at 350°F (175°C) for 20 minutes.

Chia Seed Pudding with Coconut Milk

Ingredients:

- ½ cup (120ml) coconut milk
- 2 tablespoons chia seeds
- 1 teaspoon vanilla extract

Instructions:

1. **Mix Ingredients:** Stir all ingredients in a bowl.
2. **Chill Overnight:** Refrigerate for at least 4 hours or overnight.

Sugar-Free Peanut Butter Cookies

Ingredients:

- 1 cup (250g) natural peanut butter
- ¼ cup (60ml) sugar-free sweetener
- 1 egg
- 1 teaspoon vanilla extract

Instructions:

1. **Mix Ingredients:** Combine all ingredients in a bowl.
2. **Shape & Bake:** Form into small cookies and bake at 350°F (175°C) for 10-12 minutes.

Keto Cheesecake Bites

Ingredients:

- 1 cup (225g) cream cheese
- ¼ cup (60ml) sugar-free sweetener
- 1 teaspoon vanilla extract
- ½ teaspoon lemon juice

Instructions:

1. **Blend Ingredients:** Mix all ingredients until smooth.
2. **Chill & Serve:** Refrigerate for 1 hour before serving.

Dark Chocolate Coconut Truffles

Ingredients:

- 1 cup (100g) unsweetened shredded coconut
- ¼ cup (60ml) sugar-free sweetener
- ¼ cup (60ml) coconut cream
- ½ cup (100g) melted dark chocolate (sugar-free)

Instructions:

1. **Mix Coconut Filling:** Combine shredded coconut, sweetener, and coconut cream. Form into small balls.
2. **Coat in Chocolate:** Dip in melted chocolate and let set in the fridge.

Banana Oatmeal Cookies

Ingredients:

- 2 ripe bananas, mashed
- 1 cup (90g) rolled oats
- ½ teaspoon cinnamon
- ½ teaspoon vanilla extract

Instructions:

1. **Mix Ingredients:** Combine all ingredients in a bowl.
2. **Shape & Bake:** Form into cookies and bake at 350°F (175°C) for 12-15 minutes.

Sugar-Free Carrot Cake

Ingredients:

- 1 cup (125g) almond flour
- 1 teaspoon baking powder
- ½ teaspoon cinnamon
- ½ cup (120ml) sugar-free sweetener
- 2 eggs
- ½ cup (100g) grated carrots

Instructions:

1. **Mix Ingredients:** Combine all ingredients in a bowl.
2. **Bake:** Pour into a greased pan and bake at 350°F (175°C) for 25 minutes.

Berry Chia Jam Bars

Ingredients:

- 1 cup (100g) almond flour
- ¼ cup (60ml) coconut oil
- ¼ cup (60ml) chia jam (made from berries + chia seeds)

Instructions:

1. **Mix Crust:** Combine almond flour and coconut oil, press into a pan.
2. **Add Jam:** Spread chia jam on top and chill before serving.

No-Bake Coconut Macaroons

Ingredients:

- 1 cup (100g) unsweetened shredded coconut
- ¼ cup (60ml) coconut cream
- ¼ cup (60ml) sugar-free sweetener

Instructions:

1. **Mix Ingredients:** Stir everything together in a bowl.
2. **Shape & Chill:** Form into small balls and refrigerate for 30 minutes.

Flourless Almond Butter Cookies

Ingredients:

- 1 cup (250g) almond butter
- ¼ cup (60ml) sugar-free sweetener
- 1 egg
- 1 teaspoon vanilla extract

Instructions:

1. **Mix Ingredients:** Combine all ingredients in a bowl.
2. **Shape & Bake:** Form into small cookies and bake at 350°F (175°C) for 10-12 minutes.

Sugar-Free Lemon Bars

Ingredients:

- **Crust:**
    - 1 cup (100g) almond flour
    - ¼ cup (60ml) melted butter
    - 2 tablespoons sugar-free sweetener
- **Filling:**
    - ½ cup (120ml) lemon juice
    - ¼ cup (60ml) sugar-free sweetener
    - 2 eggs

Instructions:

1. **Prepare Crust:** Mix almond flour, butter, and sweetener, press into a pan, and bake at 350°F (175°C) for 10 minutes.
2. **Make Filling:** Whisk lemon juice, sweetener, and eggs, pour over the crust, and bake for 15 minutes.

Cinnamon Baked Apples

Ingredients:

- 2 apples, sliced
- 1 teaspoon cinnamon
- 1 tablespoon melted butter

Instructions:

1. **Toss Apples:** Mix apple slices with cinnamon and butter.
2. **Bake:** Roast at 375°F (190°C) for 20 minutes.

Chocolate Chia Pudding

Ingredients:

- ½ cup (120ml) unsweetened almond milk
- 2 tablespoons chia seeds
- 1 tablespoon unsweetened cocoa powder
- 1 teaspoon vanilla extract

Instructions:

1. **Mix Ingredients:** Stir all ingredients in a bowl.
2. **Chill Overnight:** Refrigerate for at least 4 hours or overnight.

Sugar-Free Pumpkin Pie

Ingredients:

- **Crust:**
    - 1 cup (100g) almond flour
    - ¼ cup (60ml) melted butter
    - 2 tablespoons sugar-free sweetener
- **Filling:**
    - 1 cup (250g) pumpkin purée
    - 2 eggs
    - ¼ cup (60ml) sugar-free sweetener
    - 1 teaspoon cinnamon

Instructions:

1. **Prepare Crust:** Mix almond flour, butter, and sweetener, press into a pie pan, and bake at 350°F (175°C) for 10 minutes.
2. **Make Filling:** Whisk pumpkin, eggs, sweetener, and cinnamon, pour into crust, and bake for 30 minutes.

Keto Chocolate Mug Cake

Ingredients:

- 2 tablespoons almond flour
- 1 tablespoon unsweetened cocoa powder
- 1 tablespoon sugar-free sweetener
- 1 egg
- 1 tablespoon melted butter

Instructions:

1. **Mix Ingredients:** Stir all ingredients in a mug.
2. **Microwave:** Cook for 60-90 seconds.

Sugar-Free Raspberry Sorbet

Ingredients:

- 2 cups (250g) frozen raspberries
- ¼ cup (60ml) sugar-free sweetener
- 1 teaspoon lemon juice

Instructions:

1. **Blend Ingredients:** Process everything in a blender until smooth.
2. **Freeze & Serve:** Transfer to a container and freeze for 1 hour before serving.

Almond Butter Fudge

Ingredients:

- 1 cup (250g) almond butter
- ¼ cup (60ml) melted coconut oil
- ¼ cup (60ml) sugar-free sweetener

Instructions:

1. **Mix Ingredients:** Stir everything together.
2. **Chill & Serve:** Pour into a lined pan, refrigerate for 1 hour, then cut into squares.

Sugar-Free Vanilla Panna Cotta

Ingredients:

- 1 cup (240ml) heavy cream
- 1 teaspoon vanilla extract
- 2 tablespoons sugar-free sweetener
- 1 teaspoon gelatin

Instructions:

1. **Heat Cream:** Warm cream, vanilla, and sweetener in a saucepan.
2. **Add Gelatin:** Stir until dissolved.
3. **Chill & Set:** Pour into molds and refrigerate for 4 hours.

Cacao Energy Bites

Ingredients:

- 1 cup (100g) almond flour
- ¼ cup (25g) unsweetened cocoa powder
- ¼ cup (60ml) melted coconut oil
- ¼ cup (60ml) sugar-free sweetener

Instructions:

1. **Mix Ingredients:** Stir everything together.
2. **Shape & Chill:** Form into balls and refrigerate for 30 minutes.

Avocado Chocolate Fudge

Ingredients:

- 1 ripe avocado
- ¼ cup (25g) unsweetened cocoa powder
- ¼ cup (60ml) melted coconut oil
- ¼ cup (60ml) sugar-free sweetener

Instructions:

1. **Blend Ingredients:** Process everything in a blender until smooth.
2. **Chill & Serve:** Pour into a pan, refrigerate for 1 hour, then cut into squares.

Strawberry Coconut Popsicles

Ingredients:

- 1 cup (150g) fresh strawberries, chopped
- 1 cup (240ml) coconut milk
- 2 tablespoons sugar-free sweetener
- 1 teaspoon vanilla extract

Instructions:

1. **Blend Ingredients:** Mix all ingredients in a blender until smooth.
2. **Freeze:** Pour into popsicle molds and freeze for at least 4 hours.

Peanut Butter Protein Balls

Ingredients:

- 1 cup (250g) natural peanut butter
- ½ cup (50g) almond flour
- ¼ cup (60ml) sugar-free sweetener
- 2 tablespoons chia seeds

Instructions:

1. **Mix Ingredients:** Stir all ingredients together until well combined.
2. **Shape & Chill:** Form into small balls and refrigerate for 30 minutes.

Sugar-Free Apple Crisp

Ingredients:

- 2 apples, sliced
- 1 teaspoon cinnamon
- ½ cup (50g) almond flour
- ¼ cup (30g) chopped walnuts
- 2 tablespoons melted butter

Instructions:

1. **Prepare Apples:** Toss apple slices with cinnamon and place in a baking dish.
2. **Make Topping:** Mix almond flour, walnuts, and melted butter, then sprinkle over apples.
3. **Bake:** Bake at 375°F (190°C) for 20-25 minutes.

No-Bake Cashew Cheesecake

Ingredients:

- **Crust:**
    - 1 cup (100g) almond flour
    - ¼ cup (60ml) melted coconut oil
    - 2 tablespoons sugar-free sweetener
- **Filling:**
    - 1 cup (150g) soaked cashews
    - ¼ cup (60ml) coconut milk
    - 2 tablespoons lemon juice
    - 2 tablespoons sugar-free sweetener

Instructions:

1. **Prepare Crust:** Mix crust ingredients and press into a lined pan.
2. **Blend Filling:** Process cashews, coconut milk, lemon juice, and sweetener until smooth.
3. **Assemble & Chill:** Pour filling over crust and refrigerate for 4 hours before serving.

Sugar-Free Matcha Ice Cream

Ingredients:

- 1 cup (240ml) coconut milk
- 1 teaspoon matcha powder
- 2 tablespoons sugar-free sweetener
- 1 teaspoon vanilla extract

Instructions:

1. **Blend Ingredients:** Mix all ingredients in a blender.
2. **Freeze & Stir:** Pour into a container and freeze for 2-3 hours, stirring every 30 minutes.

Dark Chocolate Almond Bark

Ingredients:

- 1 cup (150g) sugar-free dark chocolate, melted
- ½ cup (75g) almonds, chopped
- 1 teaspoon sea salt

Instructions:

1. **Mix Ingredients:** Stir almonds into melted chocolate.
2. **Spread & Set:** Pour onto parchment paper, sprinkle with sea salt, and refrigerate for 1 hour.

Vegan Sugar-Free Banana Ice Cream

Ingredients:

- 2 ripe bananas, frozen
- ½ cup (120ml) unsweetened almond milk
- 1 teaspoon vanilla extract

Instructions:

1. **Blend Ingredients:** Process all ingredients in a blender until smooth.
2. **Freeze & Serve:** Eat immediately or freeze for a firmer texture.

Chia Flaxseed Crackers with Berries

Ingredients:

- ½ cup (60g) chia seeds
- ½ cup (60g) flaxseeds
- ½ teaspoon salt
- ½ cup (120ml) water
- ½ cup (75g) fresh berries

Instructions:

1. **Prepare Dough:** Mix seeds, salt, and water, let sit for 10 minutes.
2. **Bake:** Spread thinly on a baking sheet and bake at 325°F (165°C) for 30 minutes.
3. **Serve with Berries:** Let cool and enjoy with fresh berries.

No-Bake Oatmeal Protein Bars

Ingredients:

- 1 cup (90g) rolled oats
- ½ cup (125g) almond butter
- ¼ cup (60ml) sugar-free sweetener
- 2 tablespoons chia seeds

Instructions:

1. **Mix Ingredients:** Stir all ingredients together.
2. **Shape & Chill:** Press into a lined pan and refrigerate for 1 hour before slicing.

Sugar-Free Chocolate Zucchini Cake

Ingredients:

- 2 cups (200g) almond flour
- 1 cup (240g) grated zucchini
- ¼ cup (60ml) sugar-free sweetener
- ¼ cup (60g) unsweetened cocoa powder
- 2 eggs
- 1 teaspoon vanilla extract
- 1 teaspoon baking powder

Instructions:

1. **Mix Dry Ingredients:** Combine almond flour, cocoa powder, sweetener, and baking powder.
2. **Add Wet Ingredients:** Stir in eggs, zucchini, and vanilla until smooth.
3. **Bake:** Pour into a greased pan and bake at 350°F (175°C) for 25-30 minutes.

Cinnamon Walnut Muffins

Ingredients:

- 1 cup (100g) almond flour
- 1 teaspoon cinnamon
- ½ cup (50g) chopped walnuts
- ¼ cup (60ml) unsweetened almond milk
- 2 eggs
- 2 tablespoons sugar-free sweetener
- 1 teaspoon vanilla extract

Instructions:

1. **Mix Ingredients:** Combine almond flour, cinnamon, walnuts, and sweetener.
2. **Add Wet Ingredients:** Stir in almond milk, eggs, and vanilla.
3. **Bake:** Pour into muffin tin and bake at 350°F (175°C) for 20-25 minutes.

Keto Pecan Pie Bars

Ingredients:

- **Crust:**
    - 1 cup (100g) almond flour
    - ¼ cup (60g) melted butter
    - 2 tablespoons sugar-free sweetener
- **Filling:**
    - 1 cup (100g) pecans, chopped
    - 2 eggs
    - ¼ cup (60ml) sugar-free maple syrup

Instructions:

1. **Prepare Crust:** Mix almond flour, butter, and sweetener, press into a pan, and bake at 350°F (175°C) for 10 minutes.
2. **Prepare Filling:** Whisk eggs, syrup, and pecans, pour over crust.
3. **Bake:** Bake for 15-20 minutes.

Coconut Almond Bliss Balls

Ingredients:

- 1 cup (100g) unsweetened shredded coconut
- ½ cup (125g) almond butter
- 2 tablespoons sugar-free sweetener
- 1 teaspoon vanilla extract
- ¼ cup (30g) chopped almonds

Instructions:

1. **Mix Ingredients:** Combine all ingredients in a bowl.
2. **Shape & Chill:** Form into balls and refrigerate for 30 minutes.

Baked Pears with Walnuts

Ingredients:

- 4 pears, halved and cored
- ¼ cup (30g) chopped walnuts
- 1 teaspoon cinnamon
- 1 tablespoon honey (optional)

Instructions:

1. **Prepare Pears:** Place pear halves in a baking dish, sprinkle with walnuts and cinnamon.
2. **Bake:** Bake at 375°F (190°C) for 20-25 minutes. Drizzle with honey, if desired.

Sugar-Free Mocha Mousse

Ingredients:

- 1 cup (240ml) heavy cream
- 2 tablespoons instant coffee granules
- 2 tablespoons unsweetened cocoa powder
- ¼ cup (60ml) sugar-free sweetener

Instructions:

1. **Whisk Ingredients:** Beat heavy cream, coffee, cocoa powder, and sweetener until stiff peaks form.
2. **Chill & Serve:** Refrigerate for 1 hour before serving.

Pumpkin Spice Energy Bites

Ingredients:

- 1 cup (100g) rolled oats
- ½ cup (125g) almond butter
- ¼ cup (60g) canned pumpkin
- 1 teaspoon pumpkin pie spice
- 2 tablespoons sugar-free sweetener

Instructions:

1. **Mix Ingredients:** Combine all ingredients in a bowl.
2. **Shape & Chill:** Form into small balls and refrigerate for 30 minutes.

Lemon Coconut Fat Bombs

Ingredients:

- ½ cup (125g) coconut oil, melted
- ¼ cup (30g) unsweetened shredded coconut
- 2 tablespoons sugar-free sweetener
- 1 tablespoon lemon zest

Instructions:

1. **Mix Ingredients:** Stir together melted coconut oil, shredded coconut, sweetener, and lemon zest.
2. **Chill & Set:** Pour into molds and refrigerate for 1 hour before serving.

Blackberry Almond Tarts

Ingredients:

- **Crust:**
    - 1 cup (100g) almond flour
    - ¼ cup (60g) melted butter
    - 2 tablespoons sugar-free sweetener
- **Filling:**
    - 1 cup (150g) blackberries
    - ¼ cup (60ml) unsweetened almond milk
    - 1 tablespoon sugar-free sweetener

Instructions:

1. **Prepare Crust:** Mix almond flour, butter, and sweetener, press into tart molds, and bake at 350°F (175°C) for 10 minutes.
2. **Prepare Filling:** Blend blackberries, almond milk, and sweetener, then pour into crust.
3. **Chill & Serve:** Refrigerate for 2 hours before serving.

Sugar-Free Chocolate Pudding

Ingredients:

- 2 cups (480ml) unsweetened almond milk
- ¼ cup (25g) unsweetened cocoa powder
- ¼ cup (60ml) sugar-free sweetener
- 1 tablespoon cornstarch

Instructions:

1. **Mix Ingredients:** Whisk almond milk, cocoa powder, sweetener, and cornstarch in a saucepan.
2. **Cook & Chill:** Bring to a simmer and cook until thickened, then refrigerate for 2 hours.

Sugar-Free Peanut Butter Blondies

Ingredients:

- 1 cup (250g) peanut butter
- ¼ cup (60ml) sugar-free sweetener
- 2 eggs
- 1 teaspoon vanilla extract
- ¼ teaspoon baking soda

Instructions:

1. **Mix Ingredients:** Combine peanut butter, sweetener, eggs, vanilla, and baking soda in a bowl.
2. **Bake:** Pour into a pan and bake at 350°F (175°C) for 20-25 minutes.

Mango Coconut Cream Dessert

Ingredients:

- 1 cup (240ml) coconut cream
- ½ cup (100g) mango puree
- 2 tablespoons sugar-free sweetener
- 1 teaspoon vanilla extract

Instructions:

1. **Blend Ingredients:** Mix coconut cream, mango puree, sweetener, and vanilla until smooth.
2. **Chill:** Refrigerate for 2 hours before serving.

Keto Snickerdoodle Cookies

Ingredients:

- 1 cup (100g) almond flour
- ¼ cup (50g) unsweetened erythritol
- 1 teaspoon cinnamon
- 1 egg
- 1 teaspoon vanilla extract
- 2 tablespoons melted butter
- ¼ teaspoon baking soda

Instructions:

1. **Mix Ingredients:** Combine all ingredients in a bowl.
2. **Shape & Bake:** Form into balls, roll in cinnamon, and bake at 350°F (175°C) for 10-12 minutes.

Sugar-Free Tiramisu

Ingredients:

- 1 cup (240ml) brewed coffee, cooled
- 1 cup (240g) mascarpone cheese
- ½ cup (120ml) heavy cream
- ¼ cup (60ml) sugar-free sweetener
- 1 teaspoon vanilla extract
- 1 tablespoon unsweetened cocoa powder

Instructions:

1. **Prepare Cream:** Whisk mascarpone, heavy cream, sweetener, and vanilla until smooth.
2. **Layer:** Dip sugar-free ladyfingers in coffee, layer with cream mixture, and repeat.
3. **Chill:** Refrigerate for 4 hours before serving. Sprinkle with cocoa powder.

Sugar-Free Vanilla Ice Cream

Ingredients:

- 2 cups (480ml) heavy cream
- 1 cup (240ml) unsweetened almond milk
- 2 teaspoons vanilla extract
- ½ cup (120ml) sugar-free sweetener

Instructions:

1. **Mix Ingredients:** Whisk cream, almond milk, sweetener, and vanilla.
2. **Freeze & Stir:** Pour into a container and freeze, stirring every 30 minutes until set.

Blueberry Almond Butter Cups

Ingredients:

- 1 cup (250g) almond butter
- ¼ cup (60ml) melted coconut oil
- 2 tablespoons sugar-free sweetener
- ¼ cup (40g) fresh blueberries

Instructions:

1. **Prepare Cups:** Melt almond butter, coconut oil, and sweetener together.
2. **Assemble:** Spoon into silicone molds, add blueberries, and freeze for 1-2 hours.

Chocolate Coconut Chia Bars

Ingredients:

- 1 cup (100g) unsweetened shredded coconut
- 2 tablespoons chia seeds
- ¼ cup (60ml) unsweetened cocoa powder
- 2 tablespoons sugar-free sweetener
- ¼ cup (60ml) coconut oil

Instructions:

1. **Mix Ingredients:** Combine all ingredients in a bowl.
2. **Set & Chill:** Press into a baking dish and refrigerate for 2 hours. Slice into bars.

Sugar-Free Cranberry Orange Muffins

Ingredients:

- 1 cup (100g) almond flour
- ½ cup (50g) cranberries, chopped
- ¼ cup (60ml) orange juice
- 2 eggs
- ¼ cup (60ml) sugar-free sweetener
- 1 teaspoon baking powder

Instructions:

1. **Mix Ingredients:** Combine almond flour, cranberries, orange juice, eggs, sweetener, and baking powder.
2. **Bake:** Pour into muffin tin and bake at 350°F (175°C) for 18-20 minutes.

Sugar-Free Chocolate Chip Cookies

Ingredients:

- 1 cup (100g) almond flour
- ¼ cup (50g) sugar-free chocolate chips
- ¼ cup (60ml) melted butter
- ¼ cup (60ml) sugar-free sweetener
- 1 egg
- ½ teaspoon vanilla extract
- ½ teaspoon baking soda

Instructions:

1. **Mix Ingredients:** Stir all ingredients together in a bowl.
2. **Shape & Bake:** Form into small balls, place on a baking sheet, and bake at 350°F (175°C) for 10-12 minutes.

Sugar-Free Hazelnut Fudge

Ingredients:

- 1 cup (250g) hazelnut butter
- ¼ cup (60ml) unsweetened coconut milk
- 2 tablespoons sugar-free sweetener
- 1 teaspoon vanilla extract

Instructions:

1. **Mix Ingredients:** Stir all ingredients together until smooth.
2. **Chill & Set:** Pour into a lined dish and refrigerate for 2 hours before cutting into squares.

www.ingramcontent.com/pod-product-compliance
Lightning Source LLC
LaVergne TN
LVHW081504060526
838201LV00056BA/2925